PLEASE FORGIVE ME BEFORE IT'S TOO LATE:

I Love You and I Need You in My Life

CHERYLE T. RICKS

XULON PRESS

Xulon Press
2301 Lucien Way #415
Maitland, FL 32751
407.339.4217
www.xulonpress.com

Unless otherwise indicated, Scripture quotations taken from the King James Version (KJV)–public domain.

Scripture quotations taken from the Holy Bible, New International Version (NIV). Copyright © 1973, 1978, 1984, 2011 by Biblica, Inc.™. Used by permission. All rights reserved.

Printed in the United States of America.

Paperback ISBN-13: 978-1-63221-890-2
eBook ISBN-13: 978-1-6322-1891-9

To: Karen,

Forgiveness is the gift you give yourself!!

Love

Cheryl T. Ricks
443-447-7267

Dedication and Acknowledgments

I dedicate this book to my Lord and Savior, Jesus Christ, who forgave me and loved me into wholeness, and for allowing me to help others heal through my writing.

I also dedicate this book to my children: Ronald Cowan, Jr., Chevelle Ricks, Sherelle Ricks Witherspoon, and Larry Tyrone Ricks, Jr. I pray that each of you allow God to help you overcome the pain I caused you when you were young children! I hope this book helps your heart to heal and gives you what you need from me, your mother! Time heals all wounds when we give the pain to God, and allow Him to show us how that pain creates the people we ultimately become because of it! I love you so much and I am proud of each of you!

To my sisters: Lorraine Lifsey, Marguerite Hudson, Lynda Thomason, and Frances Mealy. To my brother: Joseph James Mealy, Jr.; my brother-in-law, Herbert L. Hudson; and my sister-in-law, Pamela Mealy. Thank you all for loving me and reminding me how special family is! Your love, support, and acceptance help me know that I am a part of an awesome family! I thank God that you are my family!

To my mother: Marguerite Edna Spicer Mealy. Thank you for showing me the unconditional love of a mother and for helping me grow into the woman you knew I could be! Mom, I will always be grateful for your prayers and your faith in me! I feel your presence every day!

To my father: Joseph James Mealy, Sr. Thank you for teaching me how to help others, to be unselfish, to slow down, and look at what I was doing. These lessons continue to serve me after all these years.

To my grandsons: Kasshan L. Cowan, Diontay Braheem Ricks, Derek Defontaine Goldsmith III, Larry Tyrone Ricks III, Malik Jauan Hargis, and Cortly Witherspoon, Jr. Thank you for being the awesome young men you are! I am proud of each of you!

To my only granddaughter: Aniya Satea Whitfield. Thank you for being so wonderful! I am very proud of you!

To my dear friends: Marie Minor, Catherine Dixon-Kheir, Cheryl Ann Scott, Francis Charles Snyder, Joi Ford, Jubilee Perry, Zainabu Kamara, Aletha Falls, Ira Falls, Bonita White, and Tiny Tillman. Thank you for always being true friends and a blessing to my life. I thank God for each of you!

To my literary team: Marguerite E. Hudson, Marie Minor, Deacon Austin L. Patterson, III, Chaplain Samuel L. Smith, Aletha Falls, attorney Cheryl Ann Scott, and Dr. Gerri Bates, professor. Thank you all for your feedback, encouragement, guidance, help, and support I needed to finish writing this book. I am forever grateful to all of you!

TABLE OF CONTENTS

What Is Love:

1 CORINTHIANS CHAPTER 13:1-8A, 11 AND 13
New International Version

If I speak in the tongues of men or of angels, but do not have love, I am only a resounding gong or a clanging cymbal. If I have the gift of prophecy and can fathom all mysteries and all knowledge, and if I have a faith that can move mountains, but do not have love, I am nothing. If I give all I possess to the poor and give over my body to hardship that I may boast, but do not have love, I gain nothing.

Love is patient, love is kind. It does not envy, it does not boast, it is not proud. It does not dishonor others, it is not self-seeking, it is not easily angered, it keeps no record of wrongs. Love does not delight in evil but rejoices with the truth. It always protects, always trusts, always hopes, always perseveres. Love never fails…

When I was a child, I talked like a child, I thought like a child, I reasoned like a child. When I became a man, I put the ways of childhood behind me… And now these three remain: faith, hope and love. But the greatest of these is love.

THE FOREWORD
By Dr. Gerri Bates

In the fall of each academic year, the young, energetic high school graduates of the previous spring head for the hallowed halls of higher education, taking the beginning steps of adulthood and choosing the paths they will ultimately follow. Cheryle, an atypical older student, came to the campus of Morgan State University, having already experienced some of the thrashings of life as examples that she would later use to assist others in finding their way to better circumstances. As her professor, I observed that she had a quiet and understanding spirit: determined to achieve, always positive in attitude, never negative in purpose or action. I could see the good in her, the ability to attract rather than repel. After studying with me for four classes and staying in contact with me after graduation, I got to know her personally and intimately, witnessing her trust in God and her faith in the Word of God in her life. Therefore, I have concluded that as a student, she was laying the groundwork for her future endeavor of composing in the genre of Christian writings, that would bless those in search of answers to some of life's issues. I am delighted to write this foreword, because I can honestly state that she is God-minded and God-centered; a passionate student of the Word of God and His promises made. I especially draw inspiration from Cheryle's writings on forgiveness, my personal distraction to living my best life. This book is a valuable contribution to the scriptural teachings that illustrate an almost methodical process to forgiveness, according to the Holy Scriptures.

Do you know the feeling of going through life daily with a heavy heart? This feeling is burdensome, attaching itself and sucking the life's blood as leeches do. I have wrestled for more than thirty years with the matter of forgiving a family member whom I feel wronged me, hurt me severely, assassinated my character, and scandalized my name. I have been preoccupied with the lies that my family member told on me and the opportunities taken to engage any willing listener to believe the accounts told. I cut off all contact, communication, and interaction with my family member, turning myself into a victim, suffering daily and enduring great loss. Betrayal is difficult to bear, but my life will not manifest the promise of God until I act on the promise that God has given me. Thirty years is a long time to hold a grudge—too long. In Cheryle's book, I learned that the Word of God teaches to cast all burdens on the Lord who will sustain me, as well as to follow goodness and mercy all the days of my life, which is a beginning course of action to learn to forgive.

Why do I think I am going through something that God does not understand? When Jesus was crucified on the cross by those who refused to accept Him or acknowledge Him as Christ, "He told the Father to forgive them because they know not what they do," (Luke 23:34, KJV). All manner of mankind was represented among the tormentors, even those who demanded that He show them proof of His role and existence. They alienated and separated themselves from God, causing spiritual separation from the Life-giver. In that sense, I am taking responsibility for my own chance to be set free as a captive when the responsibility is not mine. Jesus took the first step; He already arranged forgiveness. All I am expected to do is follow His teachings. He did not wail and moan over the things the people did to Him. Instead, He forgave them and petitioned the Father to forgive them also. Cheryle's writings showcase that God heals the hurting places, making the pain dissipate, but I must follow His teachings. I cannot be the judge proclaiming justice for myself because I think my sentence for others is fair. I must speak forgiveness to make the pain go away. Cheryle's writings give full voice to the Word of God and construct a necessary realization of the need to adhere to the Word of God on forgiveness.

Why do I think I am not supposed to endure offenses? Everyone gets offended sometime; without offenses, there cannot be any growth to the next level. The greater the offenses are, the greater the growth becomes. If I want to be forgiven, then I need to learn to forgive. The Word of God teaches us in Matthew 6:14(KJV), "if I forgive others of their transgressions, my Father in heaven will forgive me." Into my life I need to bring love, tenderness, and kindness. The greatest of these is love," (1 Cor. 13:13 NIV). Cheryle's writings are abundantly clear that God wants the best for us always. The guidance that is needed to live this life and prosper is found in His word. Jesus is the conduit through which we have life and a pathway back to God.

God is willing to forgive all who call on Him. He will restore an aching heart. Cheryle informs us that relationships can be forgiven, but not all relationships can be restored. The priority is to forgive and then move on. Do not become preoccupied with the ills of failed relationships. Mess happens. Forgive those who trespass against us, cast our cares on the Lord, and allow God to work miracles in our lives. Do not dwell in the past, but look forward to new things happening in life that do not make us double over in pain. Holding on to old hurts and pains impedes our progress. We need to let that old stuff go and ameliorate ourselves to the goodness God has to offer. We do not have to become spiritually, emotionally, or morally bankrupt. All we need to do is keep our hearts open to God and seek the desires of His heart, so that we may benefit from His truth, mercy, and understanding. If we walk in forgiveness, God is always open to forgive us.

Thus, Cheryle's book is a roadmap to forgiveness. She details the various ways in which God offers forgiveness. She explains that through an accumulation of hurt, pain, weakness, and error, we can turn from our wicked ways and seek the face of God, heed to His Word, forgive others, and reap the benefits of God's promises. Imagine all we need to discover the heart of God is to forgive every offensive act.

Dr. Gerri Bates, Professor
Bowie State University

Preface:

THE CHERYLE T. RICKS' STORY PART THREE

LIFE! As I mentioned in my first two books, *Sister Circle: The Power Of Sisterhood – A Guide To Becoming The Woman God Designed You To Be* and *Rest In God: How To Keep Living When Life Gets Hard,* we can live through the most difficult things and find a way to keep living and enjoying our lives, only to find that the people in our lives have not gotten through any of the things we have overcome. I have the best children, grandchildren, and siblings a person can ask for! They are unique and special in their own way. Each of them add something wonderful to my life, but they don't know it.

My children went through everything I survived: domestic violence abuse, a mental health breakdown, lack of self-esteem, foreclosure of my home, breast cancer, skin cancer, being sued by a debt collector, and bankruptcy. However, they have not healed from any of the pain that I have caused them.

I was trying to get on the other side of everything that I was going through by letting God help me live an amazing life, in spite of having a mental health diagnosis. You see, I was diagnosis with bipolar disorder in 1989, but I have not had a mental health episode or been in a mental health hospital in over twenty-eight years. I am currently the president, founder, and CEO of The Women Empowerment Circle, LLC. I am also a motivational speaker, a poet, an evangelist, and the author of two life-changing books. Prior to starting my first business in 2013, I worked as a paralegal for the state of Maryland for just under twelve years. To prepare for my career as a paralegal, I interned with the Juvenile Justice Department, the Public Defender's Office, the State Attorney's Office-Domestic Violence Unit, and the Legal Division of Department of Social Services for Baltimore City. I have completed mediation, domestic violence, and HIV/AIDS trainings.

In 2001, I earned my Associate of Arts Degree as a Legal Assistant from Baltimore City Community College. On December 17, 2004, I went to settlement to buy my first home. In 2009, I brought my first car and

I earned my Bachelor's Degree in Management from Morgan State University.

As you can see, my relationship with God has allowed me to live a wonderful life in spite of everything I have been through. I have achieved a lot, but I have lost much more. You see, my children are still feeling the loss of their mother when I left them with their father for two years when they were little children. I am so proud of my children for raising their children and making a good life for themselves and their families, in spite of not having me in their lives or their children's lives.

I thought overcoming the challenges I faced and making something out of my life was enough to give my children. However, at times, I thought it would have been easier for my children to forgive me if I were a drug addict or stayed mentally ill. That way, I would have had a good reason for not giving them what they need from me.

My children have been very supportive to me in so many ways over the years, in spite of the pain they have in their hearts. I never allowed myself to see that their pain was caused by my inability to help them work through not having the mother they so desperately needed. It is so painful to have the world embrace me and my children reject me! For years, I have been feeling the same pain that my children have been feeling. However, I didn't realize it until now. My children and I have been going through life trying to make do without the three things we need from each other: acceptance, forgiveness, and unconditional love!

As of the writing of this book, my children and I have been on individual journeys to deal with the issues and pain that we've experienced in our lives and in our relationships with each other. Because of this, my children and I have been able to express our feelings to each other and continue the long needed conversation about how they were affected when I left them with their father for two years. God helped us to discover our true selves and process those things that have hindered us from moving towards our hopes and dreams and the beautiful relationships we desire with one another.

The love my children and I have for each other is now freely flowing because we were able to forgive each other and not blame one another for the decisions we made in our lives that brought so much pain and suffering.

During the Covid-19 pandemic, my four children and I were able to come together as a family and enjoy one another for who we are today. Everyone was relating to each other as the new people we are now and not the people we used to be! We had an amazing time during a family gathering. No one took a cigarette break nor did anyone drink a beer. Our relationships with each other are growing so beautifully and we are enjoying every moment. Since that first gathering, we have had a couple more outings and many more conversations that have allowed us to truly enjoy our relationships with each other. The book you are holding is designed to help you and the people you love to finally heal and forgive each other so your love can flow again.

Introduction

It is not just my family, but people everywhere are hurting! I have been traveling and meeting people for many years, and the one thing I have continued to see is families and friends who have ended their relationships with someone they loved and cared very deeply for. I also saw the pain they were experiencing because they no longer had that relationship. That pain is crippling their lives and hindering them from having healthy relationships with the new people in their lives; I know because I experienced the same thing in my own life. Today, I have decided not to live one more day without the people I love and the people who love me, because I was not able to acknowledge their pain and the pain I caused them. I had to discover the pain I was feeling so I could see the pain in the people I loved. Hurt people really do hurt other people.

Life is too short to live without love! When love stops flowing, bitterness, resentment, and unforgiveness come into our lives, bringing pain and heartache that interferes with the blessed lives God intended for all of us to live. The pain of missing the people we love outweighs the pain that makes us stop loving them. There is nothing like having someone you care about suddenly die without any warning and you never took the time to forgive him or her, or ask for the person's forgiveness, or just tell the person how much you love and appreciate him or her. Have you ever had a friend or family member stop speaking to you for some reason? Have you ever needed or wanted something from someone, and the person did not give it to you; and you spent the rest of your life reliving that moment you experienced that unmet need or pain? I am writing this book to help my family and your family heal the relationships with each other by sharing our pain, our misunderstandings, and our needs, so we can mend our hearts and fill the void that is missing in our lives.

Chapter One:

YOU AND ME

You are very special to me; I love you and I need you in my life! Each of us is unique and wonderful in our own way. We give one another something that only we can give. Therefore, we must be present in order to give that special something. However, because of animosity and unforgiveness, the love we have for some of the people in our lives is being hindered, and it has left us feeling hurt and devalued.

Your love feeds my soul! When you love me and you let me love you, my world is alright! Just knowing that you want to share your life with me makes me feel wanted and needed. Your presence gives me safety and assurance that you will always be a part of my life, during the good times and bad times. I never had to guess about whether you were in my corner or not. Our love was flowing very nicely until you started demanding expectations of me I could not give or didn't know how to give. I accepted you for who you are, but you did not do the same for me. When we look to others to give us what we can give ourselves, we make others responsible for our happiness and well-being, which is unfair and impossible to do.

I love you and I celebrate who you are! You have been a great blessing to me. The things you added to me and my life helped me grow and become a better me. You helped me to see myself in a more positive way, which allowed me to grow into the person I am today. I could not have gotten where I am in life without all the wisdom and insight you have shared with me over the years. If you allowed yourself to see, you would notice I did all of those things for you as well. We have been there for each other in so many ways. I have seen your struggles and tried to help you work through them, but you pushed me away and tried to fix them on your own. When you isolated yourself from me, you took away the best part of my life: YOU!

Relationships are built over time with lots of sharing and caring. Sometimes we find ourselves in difficult places, and that pain can cause us to strike out at others who have not caused the pain we are feeling. Throwing away a caring and rewarding relationship because someone doesn't do the one thing you needed or wanted the person to do is like "cutting off your nose to spite your face." Learning how to step away from people when we are not being our best selves will allow us to get ourselves together, so we don't hurt other people and stop others from hurting us.

Chapter Two:

WHAT HAPPENED
TO OUR LOVE?

C an you love me without making me you? One of the challenges we face as people is unrealistic expectations. I'm not perfect and neither are you. I never asked you to be anyone but the real you. I accept that we are different and we have flaws. When one of us asks the other to be perfect while we are imperfect, it causes pain for both of us. When we accept each other's flaws and shortcomings, we take the pressure off of both of us to have perfect performances.

I love you the way you are; please love me that way too. I can only be me, no matter how badly you need me to be someone or something else. Requiring me to be like you, think like you, or feel what you feel is like asking a fish to stop swimming in the water and fly like a bird in the sky. I love you because you add something special to my life that I don't have, and I do the same for you. I have learned no one can be a hundred percent of what we need them to be. However, we did give each other more than seventy-five percent of what we needed. Somehow, that missing twenty-five percent was more important to you than the seventy-five percent we were enjoying from one another. My life feels empty without the love and support you gave me for so many years. I need you and want you in my life, but I don't know what to do to fix what has caused us to stop speaking to each other! I know how much we meant to one another; I know you are missing my love and support too. When we met, we were the friends we prayed to God for. You were so strong and confident; I was shy and insecure. You helped to see my worth; I was the one who celebrated with you and was genuinely happy for all of your accomplishments. Before you came into my life, I did not know I was capable of being who you helped me to become. We gave each other the missing piece we needed to grow. We grew together and not apart. Then life got the best of us and it broke our wonderful relationship. People (our mates, our families, or our friends) started speaking in our ears. With their lies, they convinced us to end our beautiful and genuine friendship. Needless to say, they were jealous of what we had together and did everything they could to stop us from being everything God intended us to be. We let their lies overshadow the truth we knew about each other. I have grown a lot since that time; I now have the God-given ability to see people for who they truly are and not just what they seem or tell me they are. We can restore our beautiful relationship if we are willing to do what is needed. Let's take it step by step to resolve everything that is stopping our love from flowing. We can do it if we do it together.

Chapter Three:

IT TRULY DOES TAKE A VILLAGE TO LIVE A GOOD LIFE

A fulfilling life requires healthy relationships. Many of the issues we are facing today started when we were very young. Those life-changing experiences have caused many of us to become stuck; because of this, we missed some developmental steps along the way. Therefore, things that we should have learned at different stages of our lives we did not. Many of us had to grow up too fast. We missed being little boys and little girls. Many of our teen years were spent dealing with adult issues. Now that we are "grown," there are unresolved issues in our lives.

Therefore, a lot of us have not built healthy relationships with ourselves, and we have not processed our pain. People we trusted hurt us or neglected us in some way, and that pain is still hindering us from having healthy relationships today. Because some of us are not whole, we stay in relationships that are very harmful. Our unsolved pain affects the people in our lives and causes them to feel disconnected; it also makes them feel inadequate.

Many of the issues that caused the riff in our relationships were caused by selfishness. When we have a self-centered mindset, it is all about us and only us. Other people's feelings and needs are not important. Therefore, we throw away people like we throw out the trash. Healthy relationships require love, caring, and appreciation for each other.

A friend once gave me a wall plaque that said, "It doesn't matter who you are; it's your friends that make your world." I have found that statement to be so true. I also heard it said, "If you want to know who you will be in five years, look at the people you hang around." As people, we tend to recycle the people in our lives, trying to get them to be what we need them to be today. Some of us are committed to people who are causing the pain we are feeling. Because we don't assess the relationships that we are in, we hold onto relationships that no longer give us what we need. One day, when we can finally see people for who they really are, we learn they never gave us what we needed. People who have been in our lives for a long time will never relate to us based on who we have become. They will remind us about who we used be and tell us things like, "I remember when you used to do this or that," even though we no longer do those things. This is because they are still doing the same things they were doing years ago, and they are disappointed in their own lack of growth. Those types of relationships also stop us from knowing who we are today. They cause us to settle for less than what we need or want. When we stop trying to fit the new us into relationships made for the people we used to be, life gets so much better. We also find we have outgrown many of the people who have been in our lives for years. In fact, those long-time "friends" have stopped us from having new friends.

It is important to allow new people into our lives! When we make new friends, they will see us for the people we are today. They will also give us credit for all the ways we have improved. They will not know anything about our past mistakes or poor choices, unless we feel compelled to tell them. They will also celebrate us for how far we have come. Therefore, if we want all of our needs met, we must grow our circle of friends. When we open our lives up to other positive and caring people, we are able to find the things we need that could not be found in the people we have known for years. It truly does take a village to live a full and enjoyable life. A larger circle of friends also stops us from overwhelming the few people who have been there for us in times past. Enlarging our circle of friends allows us to grow and learn so much about life and how to overcome all of the challenges it brings. We learn so much about ourselves when we meet new people. What we learn most is how much we have grown, and how much better we make decisions and process the situations that come into our lives.

Do you remember when someone you met came into your life at a time when you truly needed him or her? The person he or she was; the knowledge and wisdom the person had helped you work through the challenge you were facing in that season of your life? When we recognize that all of us are limited in what we know and what we can do, life becomes a whole lot less frustrating. As we enlarge our circle of friends and acquaintances, we discover all kinds of special qualities and abilities that we never knew we had.

Chapter Four:

TELL ME
WHERE IT HURTS

What is your pain point? In this chapter, I will highlight several situations that have caused many of us to end our relationships with people we once loved very dearly. I have discovered that the relationships with our families have caused a lot of the pain that many of us are dealing with today. In families, cycles are repeated because each member of the family handles the same situations the same way everyone else did. Adults and teens alike enter into relationships without processing the hurt and pain they have. Therefore, they suffer more hurt and pain, and they also hurt others. When the pain in the relationship gets too great, they find a way to end the relationship. However, the children are the ones who are hurt the most! Because we don't seek help to process our pain, we fail to recognize our children need help coping with our life choices and decisions.

Many of us cannot get past the things that happened to us when we were children. Therefore, we drink; we do drugs; we sleep around; and we have one failed relationship after another because of it. The pain of a parent-child relationship is responsible for a lot of the violence, hate, and emotional, physical, and sexual abuse that is going on in our communities, as noted in one news report after another. Some children don't want anything to do with one of their parents because they were disappointed about how their parent handled or didn't handle a situation with their mother or father. I have met several people who are experiencing mental health issues from incidents that happened to them forty years ago. I have witnessed how some children blame themselves when their parents' relationship ended. They felt unwanted or unloved because the other parent left them when they left the relationship with their other parent. This is not true; however, it is true to the child who is suppressing the pain.

Some parents can be very controlling about how their children should live their lives. When their children refused to live their lives the way the parent wanted them to; or the children's life choices are against what the parents' religious beliefs are; or they failed to choose the career their parents wanted them to pursue, the parent disowned them.

Moreover, many children don't get the professional help they need growing up, which lead them to struggle all of their lives reliving the time that made them feel unwanted or unworthy of their parents' love. Then, the cycle starts all over again. Many of the hurt children grow up and cause their children the same pain they felt when they were children, but in a different way. They fail to give their children the emotional support they need, because the coping instruments they used might be drugs, alcohol, sex, work, or busyness. This is how they self-medicate themselves, instead of getting the help they need to work through the pain that steals the life they really want to live.

Their children look to them for sound advice, support, guidance, and direction, but they are unable to provide it because their childhood pain has become their constant companions. Their children also desire a relationship with them, but they give them stuff instead. Sometimes the hurting parent becomes a functioning addict or alcoholic, so it is no wonder that some of their children become addicted to drugs and alcohol as well.

Sibling rivalry, which is a type of competition or animosity among siblings, whether blood-related or not, has caused more pain than you could imagine. One sibling seems to be favored by one parent, so he or she receives extra gifts, privileges, less punishment, and more quality time; while the other sibling seems to be invisible and receives none of what the favored sibling enjoys. This child feels unloved, unwanted, and inadequate, carrying that feeling throughout his or her life. The other sibling measures his or her life and accomplishments against the favored sibling, so much so that the sibling often fails to be successful in life. Sometimes, the rivalry is intensified by one sibling taking the other sibling's boyfriend or girlfriend.

This kind of pain is felt throughout the whole family, as the nieces, nephews, and grandchildren may not be allowed to have a relationship with each other because their parents were not forgiving toward each other.

Some of the pains people are feeling were caused by the inability to love themselves. When we look to others to give us what we can give ourselves, we get hurt and offended; we then feel rejected and unloved. The lack of self-love is the greatest cause for all of the hate and abuse in the world. We want someone to love us when we don't love ourselves. Self-love is required before someone can love us. We look to others to make us happy. We want others to buy us nice things, take us to wonderful places, and treat us like we are special, while hating ourselves. Some of us love out of obligation and not because we want to. This is an empty kind of love. The person who loves out of obligation or just to have somebody will always feel unloved, because real love comes back to us when we love from our hearts.

Chapter Five:

LET THE HEALING BEGIN

U nfulfilled dreams can make us bitter and resentful; it can also cause us a lot of pain. Some of us live our lives through others by helping them achieve their dreams. We get behind the vision they have for their lives. We even plot the course to make it happen. However, we cannot see the visions for our own lives. We often disqualify ourselves from lives that we can readily see for others. Many of us live our lives in the past; the pain from the past keeps us from moving forward. We are unable to break free. Some of us are full of shame for what others have done to us. Many of us blame ourselves for things we have done, or for things that were not in our power to do.

When we relive past hurts, it hinders us from seeing that the future can be bright and full of happiness. Every day, we replay what others have done to us and we refuse to let our abusers off the hook. We tell ourselves if I forgive my abuser, it will mean what the person did to us is okay. Therefore, we do not forgive. We think that we are punishing the person who has hurt us. The pain we feel has convinced us the person who hurt us is hurting too. We drink the poison and hope the other person dies. If we don't forgive, that pain turns into unforgiveness; and unforgiveness is a prison we put ourselves in, and some of us are serving a "life sentence." What we don't realize is we have the only key to our prison door. Unforgiveness poisons our hearts and stops the flow of love, which causes our lives to become bitter. The truth is the moment we forgive someone is the same moment the healing starts in our hearts. Therefore, take this time to forgive anyone who has ever hurt you and give your pain to God, and let Him heal your aching heart.

Some of us are blaming ourselves for what others have done to us or for what we have failed to do. It is not your fault that someone hurt or abused you! The problem was with the other person and not with you! Take this time to also forgive yourself. We have all made mistakes and bad choices. I repeat, none of us are perfect, and all of us are doing the best we know to do. So, stop punishing yourself for what you didn't do. We cannot go back in time and change the past. Wherever we are in life, we can only do what we know to do at that time. The best thing we can do is to learn as we go and do what we know. Let us resolve those things that keep causing the pain. Seek knowledge and wisdom from God, and allow Him to take us through the healing process. He will turn your pain into your message.

Chapter Six:

LOVE ME FOR WHO I AM TODAY

Time can heal almost everything. Many of us have changed for the better and we have learned from our mistakes. Therefore, stop treating people like the people they used to be. Most of us are brand-new people. We have grown in many ways since we were last in each other's lives. We do things a whole lot differently then we used to. When we were young, we did a lot of stupid and immature things because we had not learned the right things to do. I have learned that age does not mean maturity; nor does it mean we are cognitively or emotionally developed. Because of the trauma that many of us have experienced, a lot of us are unable to function to our fullest ability.

When we can forgive the twenty-three-year-old person who is now more than forty years old, we will be able to have an amazing relationship with one another today. If we can remember who we were when we were twenty-three years old and give ourselves credit for growing into the wonderful people we are today, we can enjoy something very special together.

Some of us are still holding grudges and unforgiveness toward some of the children we grow up with. I remember someone saying to me that she hated her seventy-year-old sibling because her sibling was mean to her when they were kids. However, she decided to help her seventy-year-old sibling because she stated that she would help any human being that needed the help her elderly sibling needed. When we hold things against each other for just being kids, we miss all of the benefits that our adult siblings can add to our lives. I'm happy to report that person and their seventy-year-old sibling are enjoying an amazing friendship today because they started their new relationship from today and didn't try to go back and change the people they were as children.

Chapter Seven:

UNFORGIVENESS HURTS EVERYTHING

Living upset and angry cripples other areas of our lives. In order to have happy and meaningful lives, we must have good mental and physical health! Almost every relationship will be able to be repaired if the people in the relationships work through their individual issues and the hurt the other person has caused them. However, some people refuse to get any type of professional help because they feel they would be viewed as "crazy" if they did, even though their mental health issues are keeping them up at night and stopping them from enjoying their lives.

People who don't get help for their minds become "crazy"! We have bodies, but our minds control our bodies and create the lives we have! People who take care of their mental health are mentally, emotionally, and socially healthy! It works just like being physically healthy. If we eat healthy food, sleep well, exercise, and see our doctor when you are having an issue in our bodies, we will be physically healthy. For example, if we avoid getting help for pain in our bodies, when we finally go to the doctor to check it out, we learn we have an incurable disease that is in the final stages. The doctor then tells us that he could have cured our disease if we had come to see him when we first noticed the pain in our bodies.

Therapists, psychiatrists, and psychologists help us keep our minds healthy so our lives can become happy and enjoyable. Good mental health allows us to learn how to work through the challenges in life and discover who you are! When we cannot process the challenges, problems, and stresses we encounter, we become walking time bombs, waiting for the final straw that takes away our sanity. This is the reason there is so much violence, murder, and suicide! When we, as human beings, realize that we cannot fix any of our problems and challenges on our own, some of us will stop self-medicating with drugs, alcohol, sex, video games, and mindless TV, and get the help we need and care less about what people think about us. Truth be told, people call us "crazy" because sometimes we are acting like we are mentally unstable. How long are we going to let the pain of our pasts hold us hostage and stop us from enjoying our lives? When are we going to get sick and tired of being sick and tired of living lives that deprive us of the life we really want and deserve? If we can't do it for ourselves, do it for the people who are trying to love us!

Chapter Eight:

ALL RELATIONSHIPS CAN BE FORGIVEN, BUT NOT ALL RESTORED

I s your relationship a true friendship? A lot of us call people a friend without allowing the person to earn the title of friend. Some of us are so lonely or desperate to have someone to walk the journey of life with us that we make friendships with people who don't have any of the important qualities a friend requires. A tried and tested friendship is the best relationship there is! The love, acceptance, appreciation, support, and encouragement we provide for each other over the years have given both of us awesome lives. We have spent thousands of hours talking and sharing our hopes, dreams, celebrating the highs, and helping each other through the lows. We became the confidant each other needed to work through the hard and painful places in our lives. Our friend has been an anchor that kept our lives from becoming too much to bear. Our friend helped us see the better parts of ourselves and showed us wonderful things about ourselves we never knew. Our friend believed in us until we could believe in ourselves. Together, we accomplished many of our goals and dreams. Most of us would do something for a friend that we would not do for a family member; that's because we have invested a lot to develop our amazing friendship. Let us remember the person who hurt us is a true friend who loves and accepts us just the way we are.

When our true friend disappoints us, betrays our trust, fails to help us with something we desperately need, or is not what we need them to be, remember our friend loves us unconditionally and he or she means us no harm. We should allow ourselves to feel the hurt and the anger for as long as we need to. But, don't rehearse what our dear friends do to us by repeating it to everyone we know. We can give our dear friends some grace and mercy by allowing them to be imperfect and giving them a chance to make things right with us.

However, life has a way of changing everything, even our dearest relationships. One day things seem alright, and then we notice our dear friend becoming sharp and impatient with us. We then stop talking as often as we used to and when we do talk, the conversations seem strained. If the person you are in a relationship with has not been a true friend, and the person has abused you, devalued you, mistreated you, disrespected you, and made you feel like dirt the whole time they were in your life, let that person go! Take some time alone and allow God to heal your heart and your broken spirit. Get to know who God says you are and build your self-esteem up, so you don't allow any more people like that person into your life.

Every person we know will not always be able to give us everything we need. I remember when my house was going through foreclosure. One of my family members, who was also my friend, told me she was sorry for me. Soon after my family member said that to me, I was diagnosed with skin cancer and breast cancer. I was so hurt when she said that to me that I stopped talking to her. I wanted my family member's prayers and faith to help me get through what I was going through and all I got was her pity. After I learned about the cancer diagnosis, I knew I had to be very selective about who I shared my situation with. Therefore, I only shared my challenge with other women who survived breast cancer. I still loved my family member friend, but I was fighting for my life and I couldn't have anything weighing me down or making my battle harder.

Sometimes the people we are closest to or love us the most don't always have what we need when we need it. However, God will send us the right people who have just what we need, and they are willing to give it to us.

I am very happy to say that my family member friend and I are talking again and enjoying our relationship more than we ever have. As you can see, sometimes we have to change the way to do things to keep our relationships healthy. I think all relationships need a "time-out" sometimes because we have a tendency to take people for granted and not value them for what they add to our lives. Also, my dear friend Cathy helped me to see that we don't need to throw people away. We may just need to redefine some of the relationships that we are in.

Chapter Nine:

GOD CAN HEAL OUR RELATIONSHIP

I f you want to restore your relationship with the person you love, it starts with your relationship with God. In spite of what you are going through right now, God has an awesome plan for your life. A relationship with God keeps the stress and worry from overtaking us. God is in complete control of our lives, our circumstances, and everything else in the universe. God can heal our broken hearts and repair our relationships. When we put our trust in God, it also allows us to get some much-needed rest for our bodies, minds, souls, and spirits. When all of these areas are rested, we are better able to stay encouraged and stress-free, and have the patience to wait on God to work out our situations.

However, we cannot receive the healing in our relationships without first knowing God for ourselves. We know God when we have a personal relationship with Him. God is our lifeline; He is the only one who can guide us safely through every challenge we will face in life. God's love heals us and makes us whole. Through His love, we are able to do all the work He has called us to do. Our strength, power, and wisdom come from God, as we pray and seek Him for help. God is the only consistent help available to us twenty-four hours a day, and He allows us to come to Him just the way we are. God is the one who can tell us who He created us to be. He is the only one who has all knowledge about everything. He is the one who can make the impossible possible. He has the power to work on our behalves, move the mountains we face, and start the love to flow in our relationships. God loves us so much, and there is nothing we can do to stop Him from loving us!

We start our relationship with God when we receive Jesus Christ as our Lord and Savior. Jesus gives us access to God the Father. Romans 3:23 (KJV) states, "For all have sinned, and come short of the glory of God." Sin is anything against God's Word, which is disobedience. The consequence of sin is death. If we die in sin, we will be eternally separated from God. Sin must be paid for before we can have a relationship with God.

We cannot be good enough to pay for the sin we commit against God. Sin can only be paid for with the blood of someone who has not sinned, and that person is Jesus Christ. God gave His son Jesus as a ransom to pay for the sins of everyone in the world, because God loves us so much. As noted in Romans 6:23(KJV), "The wages of sin is death, but the gift of God is eternal life in Christ Jesus, our Lord." Jesus is the only way we can get to heaven. When we accept that Jesus died for us on the cross, and He paid the price we owed to God for sinning against Him, we are saved and we become a part of the God's family. You can receive the free gift of salvation today by admitting you are a sinner. Understand that as a sinner, you deserve death. Believe Jesus Christ died on the cross to save you from sin and death. Repent by turning from your old life to a new life in Jesus Christ. Receive the free gift of salvation through faith in Jesus Christ. Pray this prayer and you will start your personal relationship with God: Dear Lord, I admit that I am a sinner. I have done many things that displeased You. I have lived my life for myself. I am sorry and I repent. I ask You to forgive me. I believe that Jesus died on the cross for me, to save me. You did what I could not do for myself. I come to You now. Take control of my life. I give my life to You. Help me to live every day in a way that pleases You. I love You, Lord, and I thank you that I will spend all eternity with You. Amen! If you accepted the Lord Jesus today, welcome to the family of God. Reach out to someone and tell him or her about your decision. Then locate a church that teaches God's Word, so you can grow and enjoy the life God has just given you. Allow God to heal you and help you live the life He has planned for you. Read your Bible daily. Meet together with other people who believe in Jesus. Get involved in a ministry group. Talk to God every day and enjoy your new life. According to 2 Corinthians 5:17 (KJV), in the Holy Bible, you have a brand-new beginning: "Therefore, if any man be in Christ, he is a new creature; old things are passed away; behold, all things are become new." Get ready for a life that you never dreamed possible. God bless you!

Now that God has forgiven you, allow God to help you forgive anyone who has hurt or abused you. For everything that did not go the way you wished it had, give it to God and let Him fix it. Allow God to fill the emptiness in your soul. Let God's love heal you and restore you to wholeness, so you are ready to receive the love God has just for you!

Chapter Ten:

DON'T TAKE THAT PAIN TO THE GRAVE

Release your pain and forgive! As people, we sometimes view our relationships based on what we want them to be, what they have the potential of becoming, or how they can be if certain things were to change. However, this is not what makes a healthy relationship. When we can see people for who they are and respect the way they see themselves, we can build relationships that will be fruitful and enjoyable. The other person has to work on their own personal development and actively take the necessary steps toward the vision he or she has for his or her life. When we learn how to create a life we enjoy and allow others to do the same, many of our relationships will become fulfilling and a whole lot less complicated. Remember, life is too short to be unhappy. Therefore, take some time to evaluate your life and all of your relationships. Then decide which relationships are worth investing in and which ones are not. Determine who adds value to your life and who does not.

As human beings, we need to release one another. Many of us have had a difficult childhood. Therefore, we are unable to handle the challenges that relationships bring. This explains why we have gone through so much pain.

As a child, forgive your parents for what they did not give you, whether they had it to give or not. They were doing what they knew to do. Just like us, our parents are going through some of the same things that we are. If you are a parent, your children are likely lacking some of the things they need from you as well. Life can be hard, and the weight of our pain can take our minds away from the people we love the most. Forgive your siblings! We are all in desperate need of approval and acceptance. Some of us have poor self-images that made us feel inadequate. Many of us were secretly abused and mistreated; therefore, we hurt one another. The pain we are dealing with can only be healed when we forgive the person who has caused our pain. That pain has stopped us from enjoying our lives long enough! I am asking you to forgive the person who hurt you. None of us can go back and do anything over, but we can resolve those things that keep causing us pain. Let us agree to start over and move forward by leaving the past in the past and redefine the relationship we want today. Ask each other for the forgiveness you both are longing for. Then identify your current needs. Let each other know how you want the other to relate to you as the relationship moves forward. Give each other a hug and let the love flow again! Then learn to appreciate the growth in one another and enjoy the relationship you always wanted!

Love is so amazing when it is freely given and received. However, life has a way of challenging our love for self and for others. Healing must take place in you and the person you love before healing can take place in your relationship with each other. You don't need to live without the people you love. Because my family and I were willing to work through our issues and seek help from God and professional resources, we healed our relationship with each other. The joy we are experiencing is amazing! Many of our relationships can be restored if we do the work needed to bring healing. However, some of your relationships will not be able to be restored. But, you will be able to create healthy and enjoyable relationships with the new people you will meet as you continue to live your life.

Each of us is very special and we are all needed. When we allow one another to be who we really are, it starts the flow of love again. It is so important to have a good circle of friends who will help us through the maze of life. When we share our pain points with each other, it ensures that each of us is being heard and valued. When we are tired of the pain, we will get the help we need to work out the issues that caused the rift in our beautiful relationship. Let us give one another credit for growing and evolving into better people so forgiveness can take place. We can stop the pain and enjoy the rest of our lives if we can learn to forgive. God gives us the ultimate love because He is love and He forgives us while He loves us. You will feel so good to be free of the prison of unforgiveness. Now you can truly receive and give love for the first time without experiencing the pain that came with it. According to John 15:13 (KJV), a friend is one of the greatest gifts a person can have: "Greater love hath no man than this, that a man lay down his life for his friends." Let us appreciate that amazing gift called a friend, and we will create a life that is more fulfilling and enjoyable than we could ever imagine. With a relationship with God, we can forgive before it's too late!

SCRIPTURES THAT HELPED ME TO FORGIVE AND LOVE AGAIN

It was God's Word that gave me the strength and grace I needed to forgive the people who hurt me and overcome the issues I spoke about in this book. They reminded me about God's love for us and how He helps us love each other. His Word also allowed the love to flow in my relationships with my family and friends that I have not spoken to in years. It is my hope you will use the following scriptures to encourage yourself when you are going through the challenges of healing and restoring the relationships with the people you love and the people who love you!

(God Never Changes But People Do) Hebrews 13:8 (NIV):
"Jesus Christ *is* the same yesterday, today, and forever."

(God Forgives) Matthew 6:15 (NIV):

"But if you do not forgive others their sins, your Father will not forgive your sins."

(Judging Others) Luke 6:37 (NIV):

"Do not judge, and you will not be judged. Do not condemn, and you will not be condemned. Forgive, and you will be forgiven."

(Forgive Others) Mark 11:25 (NIV):

"And when you stand praying, if you hold anything against anyone, forgive them, so that your Father in heaven may forgive you your sins."

(Forgive Always) Luke 17:4 (NIV):

"Even if they sin against you seven times in a day and seven times come back to you saying, 'I repent,' you must forgive them."

(Love Others) Matthew 22:39 (NIV):

"And the second is like it: 'Love your neighbor as yourself.'"

(Give Others A Second Chance) Luke 17:3 (NIV):
"So, watch yourselves. 'If your brother or sister sins against you, rebuke them; and if they repent, forgive them.'"

(Give The Forgiveness You Want) Matthew 6:14 (NIV):
"For if you forgive other people when they sin against you, your heavenly Father will also forgive you."

(God's Forgiveness Plan) Jeremiah 29:11-13 (NIV):
"For I know the plans I have for you," declares the Lord, "plans to prosper you and not to harm you, plans to give you hope and a future. Then you will call on me and come and pray to me, and I will listen to you. You will seek me and find me when you seek me with all your heart."

(God's Blessings) Deuteronomy 5:16 (NIV):
"Honor your father and your mother, as the Lord your God has commanded you, so that you may live long and that it may go well with you in the land the Lord your God is giving you."

(Fathers Be Kind To Your Children) Ephesians 6:4 (NIV):

"Fathers, do not exasperate your children; instead, bring them up in the training and instruction of the Lord."

(God Accepts You) Psalm 27:10 (NIV):

"Though my father and mother forsake me, the Lord will receive me."

(Be Good Always) Luke 6:28 (NIV):

"Bless those who curse you, pray for those who mistreat you."

(You Get What You Give) Luke 6:31 (NIV):

"Do to others as you would have them do to you."

(Let God Handle It) Romans 12:19 (NIV):

"Do not take revenge, my dear friends, but leave room for God's wrath, for it is written: 'It is mine to avenge; I will repay,' says the Lord."

(God Is Your Ultimate Friend) Proverbs 18:24 (NIV):

"One who has unreliable friends soon comes to ruin, but there is a friend who sticks closer than a brother."

(God Gives Us Mercy So Give Mercy) Ephesians 2:4 (NIV):

"But because of his great love for us, God, who is rich in mercy,"

(God Want Us To Continue To Love Others) Matthew 5:44 (NIV):

"But I tell you, love your enemies and pray for those who persecute you,"

(Forgive always) Matthew 18:21-22 (NIV):

"Then Peter came to Jesus and asked, 'Lord, how many times shall I forgive my brother or sister who sins against me? Up to seven times?' Jesus answered, 'I tell you, not seven times, but seventy-seven times.'"

About the Author

C heryle T. Ricks is the president, founder & CEO of The Women Empowerment Circle, LLC. Further, she is a mother of four, the grandmother of eight, a published author, a poet, a motivational speaker, an evangelist, and a former paralegal. She is a native Baltimorean who has lived in many different stations of life. She is an alumna of Baltimore City Community College and Morgan State University.

Cheryle has allowed God to heal her soul. She has spent many years ministering to people. Her insight enables people to get to the root cause for the emptiness that many people are feeling by helping them see the reality of their realities. Cheryle has learned through her relationship with God that there is nothing the love and forgiveness of God, and a good therapist, can't fix.

Motivated by the love of God, Cheryle shows people how to repair the broken relationships with the people they love and the people who love them.

If you enjoyed reading this book, check out my first two books, *Sister Circle: The Power of Sisterhood -A Guide to Becoming the Woman God Designed You To Be and Rest In God: How To Keep Living When Live Gets Hard* on my website below. You may also reach out to me on the same website. Happy reading!

<u>www.sisters-circle.com</u>

CPSIA information can be obtained
at www.ICGtesting.com
Printed in the USA
BVHW031951210921
617214BV00012B/97